VEHICLES

CARS

Written by Bethany Latham

Genius Kid

This edition is published by arrangement with BookLife Publishing

sales@northstareditions.com | 888-417-0195

Library of Congress Control Number:
2025943496

ISBN
979-8-89471-066-2 (library bound)
979-8-89471-086-0 (paperback)
979-8-89471-122-5 (epub)
979-8-89471-106-5 (hosted ebook)

Printed in the United States of America
Mankato, MN
012026

Written by:
Bethany Latham

Edited by:
Rebecca Phillips-Bartlett

Designed by:
Rob Delph

Photo Credits – Images courtesy of Shutterstock.com, unless otherwise stated.

Cover – UvGroup, Andrei Kuzmik, Amitav, Amateur007, Gargantiopa, Gargantiopa, UvGroup, Derek L Miller, Natdanai99, New Africa, Mo Juriaan Barends. 2–3 – VMCgroup, Nattawit Khomsanit, Natdanai99. 4–5 – Whitevector, Mo Juriaan Barends. 6–7 – Natdanai99, Matveev Aleksandr, Rob Bayer, bsd studio bsd studio, Miroshnichenko Tetiana, KS-Art. 8–9 – GeptaYs, Morphart Creation, Wend Images, Na Ta Sya, ISEN STOCKER, S.Candide. 10–11 – pixel creator, Natdanai99, Kevin Tichenor, Maksim Toome. 12–13 – konstantinos69. 14–15 – Gena96, BigTunaOnline, Mirror-Images, Everyonephoto Studio, Faiz_99. 16–17 – Sergey Merkulov, Retouch man, Naypong Studio, Kinek00. 18–19 – RGB_art, Mikhail Akimov, Bespaliy, Elizaveta Bushueva. 20–21 – Rawpixel.com, New Africa, KS concept, Lightspruch. 22–23 – PeopleImages.com - Yuri A, eurobanks, Veniamin Kraskov.

CONTENTS

Words that look like this can be found in the glossary on page 24.

CARS

Cars are amazing machines. They can help people in many ways.

Cars are vehicles used for carrying people, or passengers. Cars usually carry a smaller number of people than other vehicles.

Cars have four wheels. They travel on roads.

People use cars to drive to work or visit fun places.

Can you imagine a world without cars?

KEY WORDS

Here are some key words about cars that every genius kid should learn.

AUTOMOBILE

Automobile is another word for *car*. *Auto* means "by itself." *Mobile* means "capable of moving or being moved."

ENGINE

An engine is a machine that turns energy into movement. Most cars have combustion engines.

FUEL

Fuel is the energy source used to power a car. Most cars use gasoline or diesel as fuel.

HORSEPOWER

Horsepower is a way of measuring how powerful a car's engine is. Higher horsepower means more power.

DID YOU KNOW?

Some cars use plant and animal waste as fuel.

A TIMELINE OF CARS

Pre-Cars

Before cars, people used horses and carts to travel long distances.

1885

Karl Benz built an automobile with an internal combustion engine.

1769

Nicolas-Joseph Cugnot built a three-wheeled vehicle powered by steam.

The 1890s
Many steam- and battery-powered automobiles existed.

1888
Bertha Benz made the first long journey in an automobile. She drove around 60 miles (96.6 km).

1913
In the United States, Henry Ford made a car assembly line in his factory. Cars could be built more quickly.

Now
Many cars are powered by electricity.

TYPES OF CARS

There are many kinds of cars. They are designed to do different things.

Convertible

The roofs of convertible cars can be taken off.

Hatchback

A hatchback's trunk is part of the main body of the car. The trunk door is called a hatch.

Sports cars are usually lighter and faster than other cars.

Sports car

Sedan

Sedans have trunks that are separate from the inside of the car.

Pickup

Pickup trucks have open storage space in the back. They usually have four-wheel drive.

CAR PARTS

On the outside, most cars have the same parts.

The engine is stored under the hood.

Headlights help drivers see where they are going at night.

DID YOU KNOW?

Most cars have license plates on the front and back of the car.

The body of the car holds the passengers. It's usually made of steel and plastic.

The trunk is for storage at the back of the car.

The black outer part of tires is made of rubber.

Some cars have exhausts. This is where waste from the engine is released as gases.

IN THE DRIVER'S SEAT

On the inside, cars have many parts that help them move.

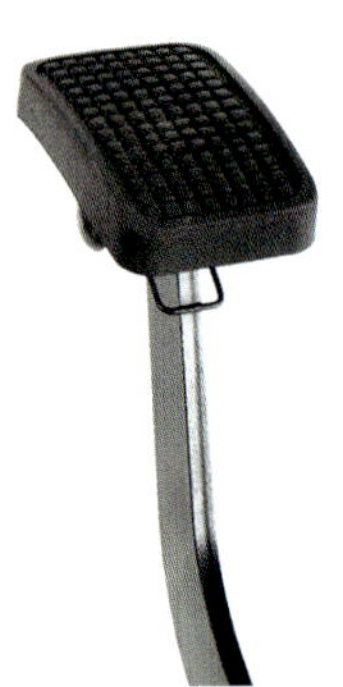

The driver presses pedals with their feet to make the car stop and go.

Pedals

The driver turns the steering wheel to control where the car goes.

Steering wheel

The speedometer tells the driver how fast the car is going. The fuel gauge shows how much fuel the car has left.

The driver changes gears using the gearshift.

Gearshift

The parking brake keeps the car from rolling forward or backward when it is parked.

INSIDE THE ENGINE

Most cars have internal combustion engines. Combustion engines use air and fuel to make small explosions. These explosions make engine parts called pistons go up and down. This makes the car go.

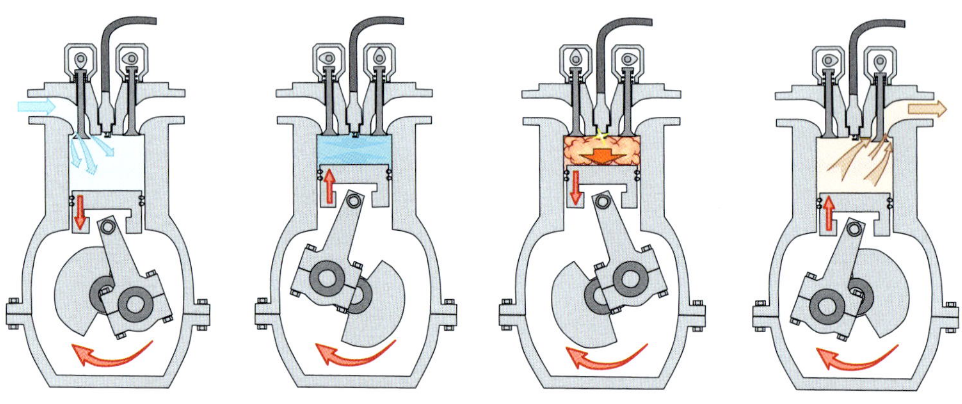

DID YOU KNOW?

Engines use heat to create movement. Motors use electricity.

Combustion engines usually use gasoline. This is a liquid mixture made from petroleum.

Electric vehicles do not use fuel in their motors. Instead, they have a battery that must be charged like a phone.

SAFETY FIRST

There are many things in a car that keep the passengers safe.

Seatbelts go across the stomach and chest. They help keep passengers safe in case of a crash.

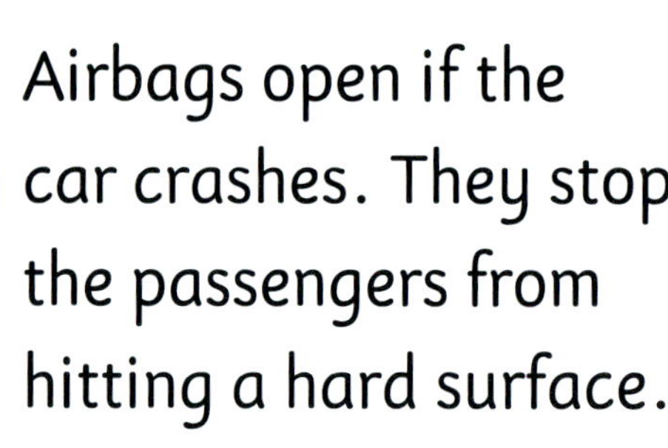

Airbags open if the car crashes. They stop the passengers from hitting a hard surface.

Horns make sounds to tell others the car is there.

Windshield wipers keep the front window clear in bad weather.

Rearview and side-view mirrors help the driver see what is behind and around the car.

BELIEVE IT OR NOT!

There are around 1.5 billion vehicles in the world. That is about one vehicle for every five people.

The first three-sign traffic signal was invented in 1923 by Garrett Morgan. Before then, traffic signals only had "stop" and "go."

It would take just under six months to drive to the moon.

Road vehicles account for most of the carbon dioxide created by all transportation. Carbon dioxide is a major cause of climate change.

ARE YOU A GENIUS KID?

Now you have tons of cool car facts to impress your friends and family with. But first, let's test your knowledge. Are you really a genius kid?

Check back through the book if you are not sure.

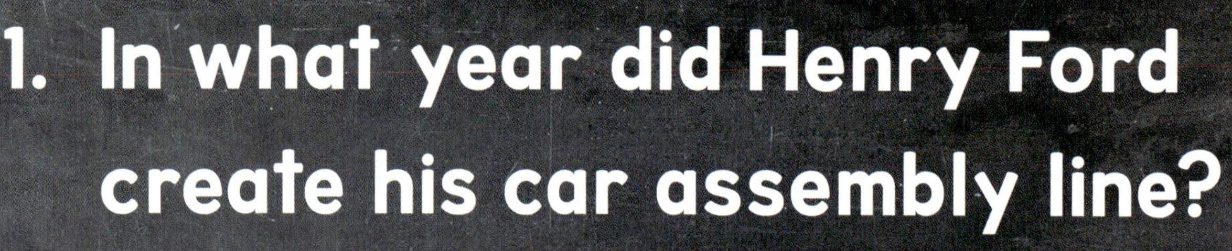

1. In what year did Henry Ford create his car assembly line?
2. What is the name of a car that can have its roof removed?
3. What is horsepower?

Answers:
1. 1913
2. convertible
3. a way of measuring how powerful a car's engine is

GLOSSARY

assembly line a line of machines and workers in a factory that each do a job to build something

climate change the long-term change in an area's weather and temperature patterns that is caused by human activities

combustion engines engines that are powered by burning or setting fire to something

four-wheel drive a system where the engine gives power to four wheels instead of two

fuel something that can be used to make energy or power something

gears parts of a machine that make other parts move; different gears help cars move at different speeds

rubber a tough material made from the sap of some plants

steam a hot gas that is made when water is heated

vehicles machines that are used to carry people or things

INDEX